First World War
and Army of Occupation
War Diary
France, Belgium and Germany

25 DIVISION
Divisional Troops
'B' Squadron 1/1 Lothian and Border Horse
28 September 1915 - 30 May 1916

WO95/2233/1

The Naval & Military Press Ltd
www.nmarchive.com
Published in association with The National Archives

Published by

The Naval & Military Press Ltd

Unit 10 Ridgewood Industrial Park,

Uckfield, East Sussex,

TN22 5QE England

Tel: +44 (0) 1825 749494

www.naval-military-press.com

www.nmarchive.com

This diary has been reprinted in facsimile from the original. Any imperfections are inevitably reproduced and the quality may fall short of modern type and cartographic standards.

© Crown Copyright
Images reproduced by permission of The National Archives, London, England, 2015.

Contents

Document type	Place/Title	Date From	Date To
Heading	WO95/2233/1 'B' Squadron 1/1 Lothian & Border Horse		
Heading	'B' Sqn 1-1st Lothian Border Horse Sep 1915-May 1916		
Heading	War Diary Of 1/1st Lothians & Border Horse 25th Divisional Cavalry From 28th September 1915 to		
Heading	25th Division B Squadron 1/1 Lothian Border From Vol I Sept & Oct 15-May 16		
War Diary	Le Havre	28/09/1915	28/09/1915
War Diary	Steenbecque	29/09/1915	29/09/1915
War Diary	Bailleul	30/09/1915	05/10/1915
War Diary	Nieppe	06/10/1915	28/10/1915
Heading	25th Division B Lothain Borders Horse Vol 2 Nov 15		
War Diary	Nieppe	01/11/1915	30/11/1915
Heading	25th Div "B" St Lothian Bords Horse Vol 3		
War Diary	Nieppe	01/12/1915	27/12/1915
Heading	1/1st. Lothians & Border Horse January 1916.		
Heading	B St: Lothian Border Horse Vol: 4		
War Diary	Nieppe	03/01/1916	27/01/1916
War Diary	Merris	28/01/1916	31/01/1916
Heading	1/1st. Lothians & Border Horse February 1916.		
War Diary	Merris	01/02/1916	28/02/1916
Heading	B Sq. Lothian Border Horse Vol: 5		
Heading	1/1st. Lothians & Border Horse March 1916.		
Heading	B Lothian Horse Vol 6		
War Diary	Merris	01/03/1916	10/03/1916
War Diary	Cantrainne	11/03/1916	11/03/1916
War Diary	Tangry	12/03/1916	31/03/1916
Heading	1/1st. Lothians & Border Horse April 1916.		
War Diary	Averdoingt	03/04/1916	22/04/1916
War Diary	Bethonsart	29/04/1916	30/04/1916
Heading	1/1st. Lothians & Border Horse May 1916.		
Heading	War Diary. Headquarters and "B" Squadron. 1/1st. Lothians and Border Horse. May 1916		
War Diary	Bethonsart	01/05/1916	09/05/1916
War Diary	Ham-En-Artois	10/05/1916	10/05/1916
War Diary	Godewaersvelde	11/05/1916	23/05/1916
War Diary	Locre	24/05/1916	30/05/1916

WO/95/2233/1

'B' Squadron 1/1 Lothian + Border Horse

25TH DIVISION
DIVL TROOPS

'B' SQN 1-1ST LOTHIAN
BORDER HORSE
SEP 1915-MAY 1916

To 5 Corps June16

CONFIDENTIAL

WAR DIARY

OF

1ST LOTHIANS & BORDER HORSE
25TH DIVISIONAL CAVALRY

From 28th September 1915 to

121/7608

25th Invasion

Mr "P" Squadron / Lothian Border Horse
Vol I

Sept. & Oct. 15
May '16

Army Form C. 2118.

WAR DIARY
or
INTELLIGENCE SUMMARY.
(Erase heading not required.)

Instructions regarding War Diaries and Intelligence Summaries are contained in F. S. Regs., Part II. and the Staff Manual respectively. Title pages will be prepared in manuscript.

Place	Date	Hour	Summary of Events and Information	Remarks and references to Appendices
	Sept.			
LE HAVRE	28	4pm	Entrain. Strength 6 officers 195 O.R.	
STEENBECQUE	29	11pm	Detrain. Marched through HAZEBROUCK to STEAM MILL farm one mile S.W. of BAILLEUL	D.C.W.
BAILLEUL	30	6am	Billeted in four farms (STEAM MILL and three farms adjacent)	
	Oct. 5		1 man to Base Hospital	
NIEPPE	6	9.30am	Headquarters moved to NIEPPE	
	7		2/Lt. McHaldane appointed A.D.C. to O.C. 3rd Divn. 2 men transfd to 3rd Divn as servants. 2 chargers transfd to 3rd Divn. 1 horse died, 2 to M.V. Sectn.	
	8	6pm	3 officers 16 O.R. to trenches for 24 hours	
	9		2/Lt. McNapier took command of M.G. Sectn. 6pm 3 officers 18 O.R. to trenches for 24 hours	
	10	6pm	2 officers 65 O.R. to trenches for 24 hours : 1 off. 12 O.R. M/G Sectn to trenches till 15th.	
	11	6pm	2 officers 65 O.R. to trenches for 24 hours	
	14		Capt. Pringle appointed to Road Control on Belgian frontier with 30 NCOs & men. Troops Nos 1, 3 & 4 moved to farm near No.2 Troop's billets, M/G Sectn to STEAM MILL	
	18		1 man to Base Hospital	
	19		M/G Sectn. moved to farm nr. Clapbank Estaminet	
	21		1 officer 16 O.R. M/G Sectn. to trenches till 27th.	

Army Form C. 2118.

WAR DIARY
or
~~INTELLIGENCE SUMMARY.~~

(Erase heading not required.)

Instructions regarding War Diaries and Intelligence Summaries are contained in F. S. Regs., Part II. and the Staff Manual respectively. Title pages will be prepared in manuscript.

Place	Date	Hour	Summary of Events and Information	Remarks and references to Appendices
NIEPPE	Oct 22		1 Offr & 3 men detailed for duty on Observation posts. Reconnaissance of approaches to subsidiary trenches. 8 horses taken on strength.	
	23		Reconnaissance of approaches to subsidiary trenches	
	24		1 charger to M.V. Sectn	
	25		Reconnaissance of approaches to subsidiary trenches. Squadron + M.G. Sectn moved to hut farms on road running NE. from STEENWERCK STN.	
	26		Ceremonial Parade. Hrh King George visits. Major W. Burton Stewart i/c A Company. Capt. Cowan and 30 NCO & men on parade. Lt. Younger and 20 NCO men on police duty in BAILLEUL	
	26		1 horse destroyed	

B. dp: Lothian Border
Home
vol: 2

12/7635

25th Kırwan

Nov 15.

Morly Blore 25th Divl Cavalry WAR DIARY or INTELLIGENCE SUMMARY.

Army Form C. 2118.

Place	Date	Hour	Summary of Events and Information	Remarks and references to Appendices
NIEPPE	Novr. 1		4 horses evacuated 30th ult.	
	3		Major W. Burton Stewart assumed temporary command 10th K.O. Yorks L.I. 1 charger struck off strength	
	4		Colonel Lord Binning, C.B, M.V.O., assumed temporary command 62nd Inf. Bde. 1 horse shot from unknown quarter, destroyed	
	5		Lt. Napier + 14 O.R. M.G. Section to trenches near St. Yves with YR Bde	
	6	10 am	Guides supplied for Canadian 1st Division's reconnaissance in 25th Divl area	
	8	9 am	Lt. Nelson and Younger conducted parties of RE and Inf. of 1st Canadian Divn on trekline in Divl area. 1 man slightly wounded (arm)	
	9		- do -	
	10		- do - 1 NCO joins Divl Bombing School as supernumerary instructor.	
	11		5 remounts taken on strength.	
	13		Officer + 14 OR of M.G. Section return from trenches	
	14		1 charger taken on strength. 3 horses struck off strength	
	17		Colonel Lord Binning, C.B., M.V.O., resumed command.	
	19		Lt. Geoffrey Williams and 1 servant joined the unit from 2/1st L'd Horse	
	23		1 horse struck off strength	
	24		Major D.A. Wauchope, D.S.O., appointed supervising officer of 25th Divl Rest Billet. Capt. A.G. Cowan admitted to hospital	
	26	10 am	Lt. Napier with 12 NCOs + men of M.G. Section reported to H.Q. 75 Bde for duty in the trenches	
			Detachments of 21st, 50th and 25th Divl Ammn Columns billeted in Nieppe attached to O.C. Divl	

Army Form C. 2118.

HQ L Ghose 25th Divl Cavalry WAR DIARY or INTELLIGENCE SUMMARY.

(Erase heading not required.)

Instructions regarding War Diaries and Intelligence Summaries are contained in F. S. Regs., Part II. and the Staff Manual respectively. Title pages will be prepared in manuscript.

Place	Date	Hour	Summary of Events and Information	Remarks and references to Appendices
NIEPPE	Nov 26		(contd) Divl Mounted Troops for Discipline.	Nieppe
	28		L/Cpl FRAME qualified at Divl Bombing School as Battalion Bomb Sergeant.	
	30		Lt NAPIER with 12 OR. returned from trenches	

"15" Sg: obermain. Rads Akten
Vol: 3

15/7938

25/10 [initials]

[initials]

Army Form C. 2118.

1/1 Lothians & Border Horse
25th Divl Cavalry

WAR DIARY
or
INTELLIGENCE SUMMARY.

Confidential

Place	Date 1915	Hour	Summary of Events and Information	Remarks and references to Appendices
NIEPPE	Dec 1		2 horses struck off strength	
	5	4 pm	Lt. C.F. YOUNGER reported to 25th Divl Bombing Officer for course of instn at Divl Bombing School	
	7	3.30 pm	2nd Army Commander inspected 25th Divl Cavalry at billets at A.12.b.4.4.	
	8	6.55 pm	Reinforcement. Temply Capt. T.D. HENEAGE, from 2nd line. posted to B Squadron with rank of 2/Lieut.	
	9		Capt. A.G. COWAN invalided home 3.12.15	
	10		1 horse struck off strength	
	12		do	
	13	1 pm	Six shells fell in NIEPPE near Headquarters billets	
	14	9 am	1 Officer & 2 NCOs conducted an approaches to 21st Divl subsidiary lines	
		9 am	do Canadian do	
	17		S.S.M. J.H. BRYDON gazetted to commission as 2/Lieut from 14.12.15	
	19		1 shell fell in NIEPPE. Col Lord BINNING, C.B., M.V.O., assumed command H/q Inf Bde with rank of Temply Brig. General	
	20		Reinforcement – 1 man posted to B Sqn. Formation of Divl Corps of Guides – Lt BRYDON + 11 N.C.Os + men detailed	
	22		Lt. G. WILLIAMS and 1 man returned to England.	
	24		1 horse struck off strength (destroyed)	

25th. DIVISIONAL CAVALRY

1/1st. LOTHIANS & BORDER HORSE

JANUARY 1916.

"B" S. Lothian: Border hours
Vol: 4

1/1 L. B Horse
25th Div Cavalry

WAR DIARY
or
INTELLIGENCE SUMMARY

Army Form C. 2118.

L A Wauch Jr Lt-Col

Place	Date 1916	Hour	Summary of Events and Information	Remarks and references to Appendices
NIEPPE	Jany 3	10 am	M.G. Section (12 men 2 guns) under 2/Lt NAPIER relieved 2 guns of 3rd WORCS in outpost trench line at PROWSE POINT - 7th Inf Bde.	
	4		1 gun of M.G. Section cooperates in combined trench mortar, grenade and Artillery demonstration against a group of dugouts in German front line trench at point marked 86 on map. 2.45pm in conjunction with above, by means of indirect fire, swept road leading to AUCHASSEUR CABT. One Canadian M.G. cooperates. Enemy Artillery vigorously replies and also flare trench front line trenches began searching for machine guns. About a dozen shells burst near R.B.H. gun. One struck the ground not ten yards from gun team but did not explode.	
	5		1 NCO to Base for discharge	
	7	10 am	MG section relieved by 8th LNL	
	12		12 remounts taken on strength	
	14		2 horses struck off	
	16		1 horse struck off	
	19		M.G. section with 2 guns took part in minor operation - 74th Inf Bde.	
	21		2 horses struck off	

1/1 L.R. Horse
25th Divl Cavalry

Army Form C. 2118.

WAR DIARY
or
INTELLIGENCE SUMMARY.
(Erase heading not required.)

Place	Date 1916	Hour	Summary of Events and Information	Remarks and references to Appendices
NIEPPE	Jany 22		2/Lt NAPIER proceeds to WISQUES for course at M.G. School 22.1.16 to 7.2.16	A W Wauchope Lt Col
	24		B Sqn M.G. Section moved to billets in Rest area near NOOTE BOOM	
	27		Headquarters moved to billets in rest area at MERRIS	
MERRIS	28		1 NCO struck off strength	
	31	10 am	Lt YOUNGER proceeds to TERDEGHEM for course at Army Grenade School	

25th. DIVISIONAL CAVALRY

Vol 5

1/1st. LOTHIANS & BORDER HORSE

FEBRUARY 1916.

1/2 L.B.Horse
25th Arm'd Cavalry

Army Form C. 2118.

WAR DIARY
or
INTELLIGENCE SUMMARY
(Erase heading not required.)

Place	Date 1916	Hour	Summary of Events and Information	Remarks and references to Appendices
MERRIS	Jany 1		1 NCO + 8 men taken on strength (draft) 31.1.16	
	5		1 man struck off ; 2 chargers struck off (Transfd 41st L.of Brig HQ)	
	7		1 man taken on strength (reinforcement) ; 1 horse struck off	
	9		Squadron & M.G. Section inspected on march past by Army Commander Interpreter struck off strength	
	10		1 horse struck off	
	15		1 man taken on strength (reinforcement) ; Sui Cross country race won by Squadron team	
	16		4 remounts taken on strength + 2 H.B. horse	
	19		Marching order parade (test) ; 1 ASC driver attached squadron for duty	
	22		1 horse struck off (evacuated)	
	19		Major H.F. CADELL from 3/1 Lt B.Horse, posted to Headqrs	
	24		Capt T.A. NELSON attached to Sui Headqrs with	
	25		1 man admitted to Hosp.	
	26		1 man attached Hqrs 21st Div - to be a.D.C.	
	28		Capt I.D. HENEAGE to England ; 1 man to England ; 1 man to R.E. (Railway Const. Co.) Major W.B. STEWART transferred to Command 10 Roy. L.D. struck off strength from 3.11.15 ; 1 charger struck off 3.11.15	

"B" Sp: Lothian Border
Horse
vol: 5

25.

25th. DIVISIONAL CAVALRY

1/1st. LOTHIANS & BORDER HORSE

MARCH 1916.

"B" Lothian Horse Vol 6

25th Div(Cavalry)
(Sheet to charge Border Horse)

Army Form C. 2118.

WAR DIARY
or
INTELLIGENCE SUMMARY.
(Erase heading not required.)

Instructions regarding War Diaries and Intelligence Summaries are contained in F. S. Regs., Part II. and the Staff Manual respectively. Title pages will be prepared in manuscript.

Place	Date 1916	Hour	Summary of Events and Information	Remarks and references to Appendices
MERRIS	March 1		2 men off strength (Evacuated to Base)	J.A. Smith Lt Col
	8		1 horse struck off	
	10	6am	Headqrs marched off from MERRIS. Joined squadron & M.G. section at BLEU. Continued to CANTRAINNE	
CANTRAINNE	11	8.30am	Continued march to TANGRY	
TANGRY	12		1553 Pte REID, D, appointed 2/Rt to be A.D.C. to Gor. 21st Divn.	
	13		Capt. A.G. COWAN rejoined. 1 private taken on strength, from Base Depot	
	14		1 Offr and 8 men attached H.Q.. XVII Corps for escort duty	
	22		Capt. J.L. PRINGLE and 31 other ranks attached a.p.m. to be trained in Road Control	
	23	9am	Marched off from TANGRY. To new billets at AVERDOINGT.	
	24		1 man to Base for discharge, time expired.	
	26		1 horse struck off	
	29		2 horses struck off	
	30		1 man to England to join Cadet School	
	31		Lieut. C.F. YOUNGER and 29 other ranks join 19th Lancers for month's training with 1st Indian Cavalry Division.	

25th. DIVISIONAL CAVALRY

VOL 7

1/1st. LOTHIANS & BORDER HORSE

A P R I L 1 9 1 6.

"B" D 1/1st Lothians + Border Horse
25th Divl Cavalry

WAR DIARY
or
INTELLIGENCE SUMMARY
(Erase heading not required.)

Army Form C. 2118.

Place	Date 1916	Hour	Summary of Events and Information	Remarks and references to Appendices
AVERDOINGT	April 3		1 horse taken on strength	
	4		2 men to Cadet School, struck off strength	
	5		2/Lt W.E.S. NAPIER + 6 other ranks attached 46th Divl Cavalry at BETHONSART for 5 days Hotchkiss course	
			1 man to England (Cadet Sch) struck off. 1 man taken on strength from Base Depot	
			1 horse struck off strength	
	8		Capt J.L. PRINGLE +21 other ranks rejoined unit from Road control duties	
	9		Capt. J.L. PRINGLE offctg Town Major, AUBIGNY - 2 horses struck off strength	
	10		20 NCOs + men proceeded to England on reengagement furlough	
			6 NCOs + men to 46th Divl Cav. at BETHONSART for course in Hotchkiss rifle fire 16th	
	13		1 man taken on strength from Base Depot	
	14		2 horses (charger) struck off strength	
	15		10 remounts taken on strength	
	16		1 man to England (Cadet Sch)	
	17		1 charger struck off strength	
	21		1 man struck off strength (to U.K. sick)	
			4 men to MONT ST ELOI for duty a/o Divl Observers	

1/1 A Store (2)
25th Div: Cavalry

Army Form C. 2118.

WAR DIARY
or
INTELLIGENCE SUMMARY.
(Erase heading not required.)

Instructions regarding War Diaries and Intelligence Summaries are contained in F. S. Regs., Part II. and the Staff Manual respectively. Title pages will be prepared in manuscript.

Place	Date 1916	Hour	Summary of Events and Information	Remarks and references to Appendices
AVERDOINGT	APRIL 22	a.m. 10.30	March off to take over new billets at BETHONSART. Personnel + horse accommodates in SE portion of village	L.A. Haigh
BETHONSART	29		940 Sergt. J. KERR assumed duties as 2/Lieut. (List No 79 of appl/s to appl by G.O.C.-in-C. dated 23.4.16)	
			Dry Canteen opened for M.Ca Y/o	
	17-30		Capt. LOCKETT, 17th Lancers, attached for training of Div: M.Ca Troops of Corps	

25th. DIVISIONAL CAVALRY

1/1st. LOTHIANS & BORDER HORSE

MAY 1916.

|SECRET|

Original.

WAR DIARY.

Headquarters and "B" Squadron.

1/1st. Lothians and Border Horse.

MAY. 1916.

"B" Lothian Horse Vol 8 25

Army Form C. 2118.

WAR DIARY
or
INTELLIGENCE SUMMARY.

Headqrs "B" Squadron (1) 1/1 Lothian + Border Horse

Instructions regarding War Diaries and Intelligence Summaries are contained in F. S. Regs., Part II. and the Staff Manual respectively. Title pages will be prepared in manuscript.

(Erase heading not required.)

Place	Date 1916	Hour	Summary of Events and Information	Remarks and references to Appendices
BETHONSART	May 1		1892 Pte Thin Sa appointed to Second Lieutenancy	
	2		1 man from Base Depôt - reinforcement	
	3		Lt CF YOUNGER and 29 O.R. rejoined from training unit Indian Cavalry Divn.	
	4		1 NCO off strength - evacuated sick	
			Working parties of 4 & 2 engaged digging trenches in 7K Bde area nights of 4th, 5th and 6th	
	9		1 reinforcement from Base Depot. 2/Lt S. Reis (ASC's B OC 21st Divn) Seconded	
HAM-EN-ARTOIS	10	7.30am	25th Bde (cavalry) left 25th Divn area to join I Corps in formation of Corps Cavalry Regt. Marches to HAM-EN-ARTOIS (north of LILLERS). Billets for night in the village. 2/Lt-Wts.NAPIER and 18 O.R. remained in 25th Divn area	
GODEWAERSVELDE	11	8.30 am	Continues march to GODEWAERSVELDE. B Sqn accommodates at two farms on GODEWAERSVELDE - EECKE Rd (Q.23.C.7.5 Sheet 27) Headqrs in GODEWAERSVELDE:	
			1 man struck off - evacuates sick	
	14		1 man off strength - to England to Cadet School	
	18		1 man off - to Base unfit for duty at the front	
	21		I Corps Cav. Regt (B Sqn + Hdqr 1/1 Lothian + Border Horse, A + B Sqns 1/1 QOR Glasgow Yeo - C.O. Lt.Col D.A.Wauchope D.S.O. 1/1 L + B Horse) less Headqrs concentrates at WESTOUTRE	

Army Form C. 2118.

Hedqrs & B Sqn 11/L & B Adre (?)

WAR DIARY
or
INTELLIGENCE SUMMARY.
(Erase heading not required.)

Place	Date 1916	Hour	Summary of Events and Information	Remarks and references to Appendices
GODEWAERSVELDE	May 21		B Sqn 2 r B Adre & B Sqn QOR had Leo billets at M.20.a.4.5 Sheet 28, A Sqn QOR.R.H.o at M.13.d.8.9 Sheet 28.	
	22	10am	Detachment of I. Gnfo.Haw. Regt. (4 off. 95 OR) to MONTREAL sector of KEMMEL DEFENCES to form nucleus garrison. 2/Lts J.H.BRYDON and J.A.THIN and 25 OR from B Sqn 2 r B H to SIEGE FARM, 28.N.16.c.7.8, as intelligence observer. Capt-J.A.Nelson + 14 o.r. to SIEGE FARM. 12 NCOs men of M.G. Section rejoined - 4 to 4 to B Sqn.	A Nelson 1
	23		7 men from Base Depot - Reinforcement.	
LOCRE	24	1pm	Headqrs moved to LOCRE. 3pm Command of KEMMEL DEFENCES passed to Lt-Col D.A.WAUCHOPE D.S.O. (Comdg I Gnfo. Haw Regt. I Gnfo.Gyclist Bn. + No 3 m.g Battery) Following troops under O.c. KEMMEL DEFENCES for tactical purposes - No 4 Coy. Royal Monmouth R.E. 1st Entrenching Bn and No 10 Bn North 2 Fusiliers.	A Nelson 1
	27		1 NCO + 14 men to B.H. to SIEGE FARM as observers.	
	30		Detachment of 2 off + 54 OR from 2nd Cav. Divn places under O.C. KEMMEL DEFENCES for tactical purposes. 3 men from Base Depot - reinforcement.	1

www.ingramcontent.com/pod-product-compliance
Lightning Source LLC
Chambersburg PA
CBHW081249170426
43191CB00037B/2100